GCSE

Oxford Literature Companions

Macbeth

WILLIAM SHAKESPEARE

WORKBOOK

Notes and activities: Ken Haworth
Series consultant: Peter Buckroyd

OXFORD

UNIVERSITY PRESS

Contents

Introduction

What are Oxford Literature Companions?

Oxford Literature Companions is a series designed to provide you with comprehensive support for popular set texts. You can use the Companion workbook alongside your play, using relevant sections during your studies or using the workbook as a whole for revision. The workbook will help you to create your own personalized guide to the text.

What are the main features within this workbook?

Each workbook in the Oxford Literature Companion series follows the same approach and includes the following features:

Activities

Each workbook offers a range of varied and in-depth activities to deepen understanding and encourage close work with the text, covering characters, themes, language, performance and context. The Skills and Practice chapter also offers advice on assessment and includes sample questions and student answers. There are spaces to write your answers throughout the workbook.

Key terms and quotations

Throughout the workbook, key terms are highlighted in the text and explained on the same page. There is also a detailed glossary at the end of the workbook that explains, in the context of the play, all the relevant literary terms highlighted.

Quotations from the play appear in blue text throughout this workbook.

Upgrade

As well as providing guidance on key areas of the play, throughout this workbook you will also find 'Upgrade' features. These are tips to help with your exam preparation and performance.

Progress check

Each chapter of the workbook ends with a 'Progress check'. Through self-assessment, these enable you to establish how confident you feel about what you have been learning and help you to set next steps and targets.

Which edition of the play has this workbook used?

Quotations have been taken from the Oxford University Press edition of *Macbeth* (ISBN 978-019-832400-3).

Plot and Structure

Plot

Act 1

Shakespeare set *Macbeth* in Scotland. The year is never made clear, but it was a time in the distant past when Duncan was King of Scotland and when the Norwegians were trying to invade. However, the play does not start with the noble characters but with three witches.

Activity 1

a) Read Act 1 Scene 1.

b) Why would Shakespeare choose to start this way? Would it not be better to get straight on with the main plot? Consider the following possible reasons and place them in rank order from most likely (1) to least likely (4).

> The audience prefers witches and spells to noble conversation, which could be boring. ` ------- `

> Plays needed to start with something striking, because in Shakespeare's day there were no lights to come down to signal the start. ` ------- `

> Witchcraft and the supernatural are important themes in the play and Shakespeare wanted to establish this by starting with them. ` ------- `

> A trivial scene at the start allows time for the audience to settle and be ready for the much more important scenes coming up. ` ------- `

c) Explain the order you have placed these reasons in. (To help with this you might like to research the opening scenes of other Shakespeare plays to see how those plays begin.)

Activity 2

Act 1 Scene 2 describes a battle between the Scots and the Norwegians.
The scene uses **exposition**, since it would be almost impossible to stage the
battle 'live'. In a series of bullet points, make notes on what happened in
the battle.

- ---

- ---

- ---

- ---

- ---

- ---

- ---

exposition key information to help the audience make sense of the action and characters
in the play

After the account of the battle, we return to the witches (Act 1 Scene 3). They greet Macbeth and Banquo, then make prophecies to each of them. These prophecies act as a **catalyst** or **inciting incident** from which the plot will develop.

> **catalyst** a person or a thing which starts or speeds up a series of events
>
> **inciting incident** an action, event or conversation that sets the plot going

Activity 3

Make sure that you know the prophecies by filling in the table below. For each prophecy, give a quotation of no more than two lines to show what the witches are promising. The final column is for you to fill in as you study the play. In it, note the act and scene when the prophecy comes true.

Prophecy (in your own words)	Quotation (the witches' words)	When it comes true
Macbeth		
1		
2		
3		
Banquo		
1		

Activity 4

a) Attention now switches to Lady Macbeth. At the beginning of Act 1 Scene 5, a significant development in the plot is revealed. What is it?

- -

- -

- -

b) After a lot of persuasion from Lady Macbeth, in Act 1 Scene 7 we find Macbeth saying: **"Away, and mock the time with fairest show,/False face must hide what the false heart doth know."**

'**False face**' and '**false heart**' are important ideas that run through the whole of *Macbeth*. List three occasions in the play when a wicked intention is masked by a friendly outward appearance.

i. -

ii. -

iii. -

c) In no more than 120 words, summarize the events of Act 1 and say what Shakespeare suggests will happen next.

- -

- -

- -

- -

- -

- -

- -

- -

- -

- -

- -

Act 2

Act 2 includes the murders of King Duncan and his servants by Macbeth. However, Shakespeare takes care to add other features that will help the plot along, in particular:

- what Duncan's two sons, Malcolm and Donaldbain, do after the murder is discovered
- the choice of the next king, given that the heirs to the throne have disappeared.

Activity 5

This is one student's attempt to detail the events of Act 2 in a flow chart.

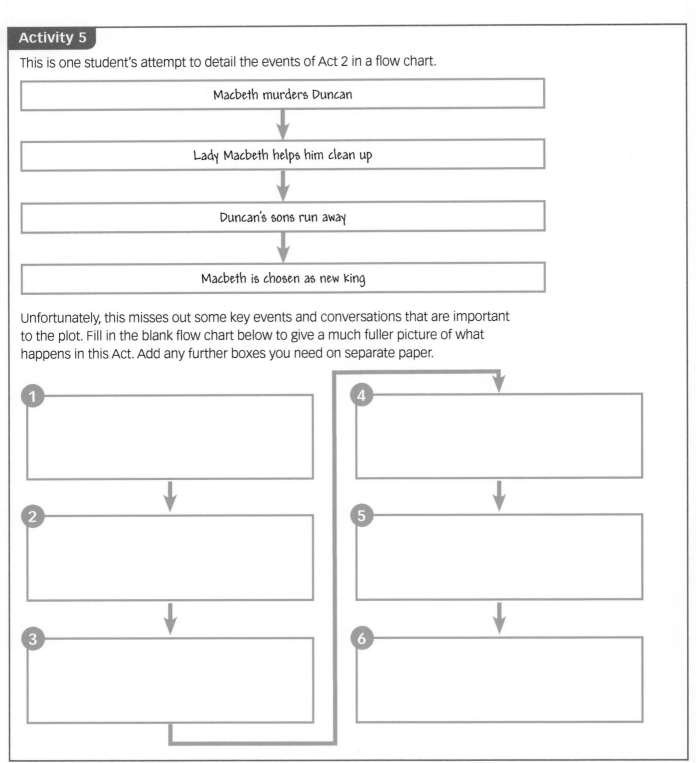

Macbeth murders Duncan

Lady Macbeth helps him clean up

Duncan's sons run away

Macbeth is chosen as new king

Unfortunately, this misses out some key events and conversations that are important to the plot. Fill in the blank flow chart below to give a much fuller picture of what happens in this Act. Add any further boxes you need on separate paper.

1

2

3

4

5

6

Activity 6

In Acts 2 and 3 the tension gradually rises. In Act 3 Scene 1 Macbeth says: "To be thus is nothing,/But to be safely thus."

How does Macbeth's thought here move the plot along?

Activity 7

Create and keep a 'tension graph' like the one below to show you how the play as a whole tightens its grip on the audience before releasing it late on in Act 5. You can add to the graph as you study the play.

Plot key points on the graph according to when they occur and how tense they are. What does the graph look like when you have finished it? It will be a good visual representation of the audience response to the development of the plot.

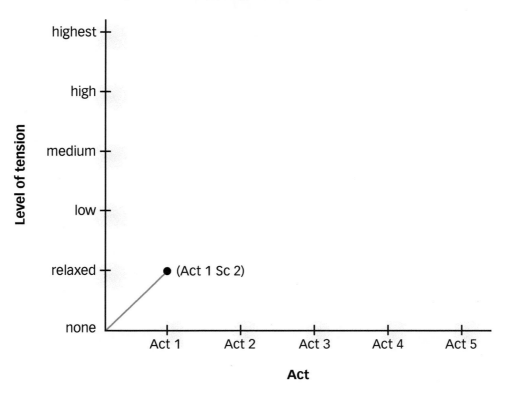

Act 3

Act 3 is full of action. Many strands of the plot are developed in the course of its six scenes. Each strand will have a bearing on the direction of the plot and indeed on how the play ends.

Activity 8

After a careful reading of Act 3, complete the following spider diagram to show how each plot strand develops.

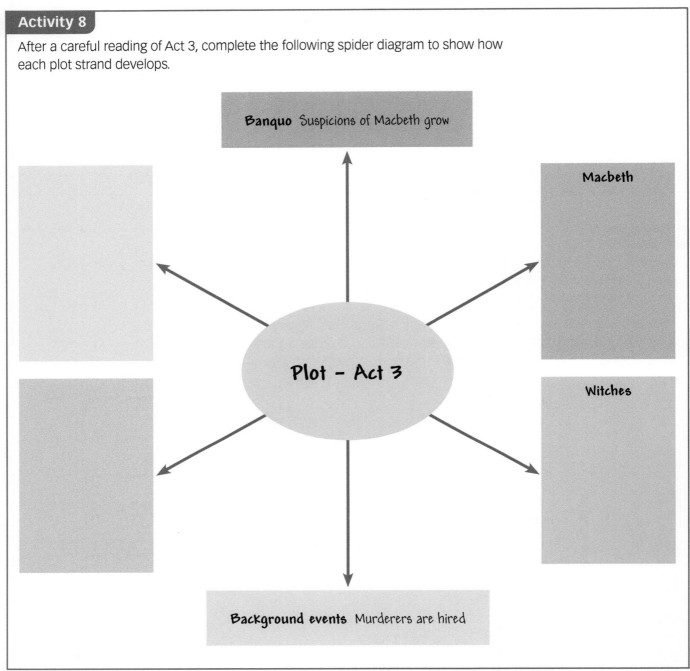

Banquo Suspicions of Macbeth grow

Macbeth

Plot – Act 3

Witches

Background events Murderers are hired

Upgrade

What happens in the play is one aspect of plot, but you should also be prepared to comment on structure. For example, Act 3 is central to the play – both literally and in terms of the importance of characters' actions. We could say that Acts 1 and 2 show Macbeth gaining the crown, Act 3 shows his kingship and Acts 4 and 5 show his overthrow.

Activity 9

Answer these questions about Act 3 to help you understand its central importance in the overall plot and structure of the play.

a) Why is Macbeth secretly plotting to kill Banquo?

----

b) Why does Macbeth stress to the murderers that they must ensure that Banquo's son, Fleance, is also killed?

----

c) How do we know that Macbeth and Lady Macbeth are very unsettled at this point in the play?

----

d) Why do the murderers fail to carry out their task properly?

----

e) At the banquet, how does Macbeth show his guests that he is guilty?

----

f) Why is Hecate angry with the witches?

----

g) What does Hecate mean when she says of Macbeth that they will "draw him on to his confusion"?

Act 4

Activity 10

Act 4 begins with the witches. Note how the structure of the play keeps moving us back to the supernatural. Why do you think this is?

Activity 11

In Act 4 Scene 1, the witches make three further predictions or prophecies. As in Activity 3, fill in the table to show what these prophecies are. The 'Comes true?' column can be filled in as you continue reading to the end of the play.

Prophecy	Comes true?

Activity 12

How do we know that Macbeth's children or grandchildren will never be kings of Scotland?

----

offstage taking place in the area of a stage that is invisible to the audience or in a location not seen that the audience must imagine

Act 4 Scene 2 is notable for the fact that we see a child (Macduff's son) murdered on stage. This indicates that the plot has taken a yet more violent turn.

Activity 13

On a separate sheet of paper, make a list of the violent incidents from the beginning up to this point in the play. Against each incident, note how Shakespeare presents it (on or **offstage**, seen or reported, mentioned briefly or described in graphic detail and so on). The first incident is done for you as an example.

Violent incident	How it is presented
1. Slaughter at the battle between the Scots and the Norwegians	Through exposition: the captain gives a report to the King.

One of the ideas running through the play is that actions have consequences. Some actions lead to one major consequence while others have multiple consequences affecting the lives of many characters.

Activity 14

For each of the actions below, identify the consequences and fill in the boxes. One has been filled in for you as an example. In some cases you might need to add further consequences as you read the whole play.

Actions   **Consequences**

Macbeth murders Duncan → Macbeth becomes king

→ Banquo becomes suspicious

Lady Macbeth returns to the murder scene to smear blood on the grooms

Fleance escapes from hired murderers

Macbeth returns to the witches to ask them questions

Macbeth has Macduff's family killed

Activity 15

a) Act 4 is short, with only three scenes. Thinking about the structure of the play, why would Shakespeare include a much shorter Act here? Put a tick against all the possible reasons below that you agree with.

Act 4 prepares us for the climax of the play by allowing us to 'take a breath'. ⬭

Although short, the Act is a micro-version of the play as a whole. It has witchcraft, extreme violence, reflection and reaction. ⬭

Shakespeare needed to get us quickly to a very exciting ending. ⬭

Tension is increased rapidly. ⬭

It does not need to be long because its purpose is to set up the play's finale. ⬭

b) Choose the reason that you agree with most and write a short paragraph stating why you feel it is the best explanation.

Act 5

Most of Act 5 concerns the final battle between Macbeth's forces and the invading army. However, in Act 5 Scene 1 we return to Lady Macbeth, who is sleepwalking. She is a character we have not seen since Act 3 Scene 4. This seems strange for a major character who was the force behind Macbeth's actions in the earlier part of the play.

Activity 16

Why do you think Shakespeare has not put Lady Macbeth on the stage in the central part of the play? In your answer, think about the play's focus and the ideas it explores at different points.

In writing about the play, always remember that Shakespeare is the craftsman who makes things happen. The characters are not real, so they cannot behave independently. Thus, it is better to say, 'Shakespeare shifts the audience's focus away from Lady Macbeth in the central part of the play', rather than 'Lady Macbeth is consumed by guilt and shuts herself away from others'.

Upgrade

resolution the ending of a narrative where problems are solved and matters are concluded

upstage the area towards the back of the stage

Activity 17

In Act 5 Scene 8 Macbeth says: **"Of all men else I have avoided thee"**.

a) Who does **'thee'** refer to, and why has Macbeth been avoiding this person?

----

b) Macbeth then says: **"[I] must not yield/To one of woman born"**. Where has this idea come from?

----

c) What is the response? (Quote the exact words.)

----

d) What effect does the response have on Macbeth?

----

e) How does Macbeth die?

The play ends with a speech by Malcolm that restores order and harmony to Scotland. The bad have been punished and the good have triumphed. This may be seen as a conventional **resolution**, but some productions choose to end with the witches silently watching as the characters depart the stage. Others have Fleance revealed **upstage** as the actors exit.

Activity 18

How would you choose to end your own production of the play, and why?

Structure

Shakespeare's plays use the conventional forms of his day. It was accepted that a tragedy should feature a great man who has a fatal **flaw** in his character. Because of this flaw, the **protagonist** is brought down. We can see in the play how Macbeth's position rapidly rises, but then just as rapidly falls.

One element of structure is the 'shape' of the play. We use the terms '**rising action**', '**climax**' and '**falling action**' to describe the play as a whole and its effects on the audience.

> *Upgrade*
>
> The structural elements of the play that you have worked on are not there by accident. They are part of Shakespeare's craft as a playwright and are as much a part of his writing as the language the characters speak. When writing about plot, remember also to comment on structural elements.

climax the highest or most intense part of the play or a turning point in the action

falling action the parts of a story after the climax and before the ending

flaw a fault or weakness that makes an object or person imperfect

protagonist the leading character in a play, novel or film

rising action a sequence of events that builds towards the climax

---

Activity 19

Here is a graph of the action of the play. Write on it events or scene numbers that you think correspond to the play's action structure. For example, 'Macbeth and Lady M discuss murder of Duncan' could come just after the start of the rising line.

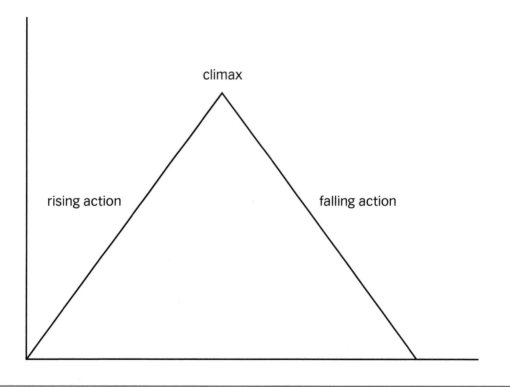

One aspect of Shakespeare's craft in structuring the play is the use of recurring patterns, often in the form of pairs. For example, the play begins and ends on a battlefield, but there is a 'mirror effect' in the structure. In the first battle, Macbeth defeats rebels who are threatening the king of Scotland; in the last battle the rebel force defeats the tyrant King Macbeth.

Activity 20

Explore Shakespeare's use of pairs and patterns in the play by making notes on the following aspects.

Kings	Wives	Royal courts	Meeting witches	Prophecies

Progress check

Use the chart below to review the skills you have developed in this chapter. For each column, start at the bottom box and work your way up towards the highest level in the top box. Tick the box to show you have achieved that level.

I can sustain a critical response to *Macbeth* and interpret the plot and structure convincingly ☐

I can show a perceptive understanding of how *Macbeth* is shaped by its context ☐

I can develop a coherent response to *Macbeth* and explain the plot and structure clearly ☐

I understand the context of *Macbeth* and can make connections between the text and its context ☐

I can make some comments on the plot and structure in *Macbeth* ☐

I am aware of the context in which *Macbeth* was written ☐

Personal response

Text and context

Context

What do we mean by 'context'? Essentially, it means looking at the time in which the play was written, what was happening in society at that time and what the important cultural events and ideas were. All of these factors have a bearing on how the play might have been received by Shakespeare's audiences and by audiences today.

The historical context

Activity 1

a) *Macbeth* was first performed in 1606. Who was the reigning monarch in that year?

----

b) How long had he been on the throne?

----

c) Who reigned before him?

----

d) The new king wrote a book called *Daemonologie* about witchcraft and magic. In the book, and in Shakespeare's day generally, witches and the supernatural were regarded as real, and as a dangerous component of everyday life that all good people must avoid. How are these attitudes reflected in the play?

In 1605, a group of Catholic conspirators smuggled barrels of gunpowder under Parliament. Their plan was to blow up the Parliament building, killing the king and almost all the English nobility, then lead a Catholic uprising and take over the throne, Parliament and hence the country. Their intended actions were foiled at the last moment and the conspirators ruthlessly pursued and executed. Since then, these events have become known as the 'Gunpowder Plot'.

It is difficult today to appreciate how profound the shock caused by this plot was. The nearest modern equivalent might be the attack on the World Trade Center in September 2001 (known as '9/11'). Shakespeare was certainly influenced by the shockwaves that rippled out from London for several years after the Gunpowder Plot.

equivocator someone who uses words or phrases with more than one possible meaning in order to be evasive or misleading

Activity 2

What echoes of the events of 1605 can you find in the play? Complete the table below.

Event in *Macbeth*	How it reflects the events of 1605
The murder of King Duncan	
The **equivocator** comments by the Porter at the beginning of Act 2 Scene 3	
The double meanings of the witches' prophecies, revealed in Act 5 Scenes 5–8	
The rightful king on the throne at the end of the play	

Cultural background

Macbeth reflects ideas and discussions that were prominent in cultural life around the time Shakespeare was writing.

Activity 3

Complete the following table by finding quotations or actions in the play that show the influence of the play's cultural context. Try to find at least three examples to support each idea.

Cultural background or idea	Quotation or action
Equivocation	"Faith, here's an equivocator that could swear in both the scales against either scale" (Act 2 Scene 3)
Kingship	
Witchcraft	
Disruption in the natural order (of people and the world)	"where we lay,/Our chimneys were blown down, and, as they say,/Lamentings heard i'th'air" (Act 2 Scene 3)

Upgrade

In their assessment, many students write about the historical facts that form the background to the play (the date, the recent change of monarch, and so on). This can be useful, but higher marks go to those who are able to bring into their analysis aspects of the social and cultural contexts as well.

Sources

In Shakespeare's time, virtually all plays were taken from stories that already existed or from historical accounts.

It was considered a compliment to the original story and its writer to reshape it into a play. Of course, playwrights took some liberties with their sources in order to make their plays more exciting, or to highlight themes and ideas that they were particularly interested in. Sometimes, plots and characters were completely changed. In 21st-century terms, the stories of Shakespeare's plays were not 'original', but the idea that stories should be original is a relatively modern concept.

Activity 4

The main source for Shakespeare's story of Macbeth was Holinshed's *Chronicles of England, Scotland, and Ireland* (1577). The extract below concerns Macbeth's first meeting with the witches. The spelling and punctuation have been modernized.

a) Highlight phrases in the extract and link them with lines from Act 1 Scene 3 of *Macbeth*. Write the lines from the play in the margins. One has been done as an example.

> Banquo:
> How far is't
> called to
> Forres?

It fortuned as Macbeth and **Banquo journeyed towards Forres**… there met them three women in strange and wild apparel… the first of them spake and said; 'All hail Macbeth, thane of Glamis' (for he had lately entered into that dignity and office by the death of his father Sinell.) The second of them said: 'All hail Macbeth thane of Cawdor.' But the third said: 'All hail Macbeth, that hereafter shalt be king of Scotland.'

Then Banquo: 'What manner of women' (saith he) 'are you; that seem so little favourable unto me, whereas to my fellow here, besides high offices, ye assign also the kingdom, appointing forth nothing for me at all?'

'Yes,' (saith the first of them) 'we promise greater benefits unto thee, than to unto him, for he shall reign in deed, but with an unlucky end: neither shall he leave any issue behind him to succeed in his place, where contrarily thou in deed shall not reign at all, but of thee those shall be borne which shall govern the Scottish kingdom by long order of continual descent.' Herewith the aforesaid women vanished immediately out of their sight.

b) Although Shakespeare uses many of the words and phrases directly from his source, what changes has he made to ensure that the scene is more dramatic when acted?

Kingship

One of the contextual elements running through the play is the nature of kingship. It is likely that Shakespeare wrote the play knowing that the king would be in the audience of one of the first performances. He therefore explores what it is to be a good king (as well as a bad one).

In Shakespeare's time many people thought that the king ruled by divine right.

Activity 5

a) What does the phrase 'the divine right of kings' mean?

----

b) What view of Malcolm as a potential king is given in Act 4? Choose one of the following, and provide evidence for your choice.

   i.   He is unlikely to become a competent king of Scotland.

  ii. There are major flaws in his character that will make his rule as bad as Macbeth's.

 iii. He will prove to be a noble king with a deep love of Scotland.

 iv. He pretends to be good and virtuous but in fact will rule by fear, violence and greed.

----

c) There are references in Acts 4 and 5 to the English King Edward the Confessor. How is he contrasted with Macbeth?

----

d) The final speech of the play is spoken by the soon to be crowned king of Scotland. Complete the table below, showing how each quotation relates to restored order or peace.

Quotation	How is it related to restored order or peace?
"we [will] reckon with your several loves/And make us even with you"	Those who have helped Malcolm will be well rewarded
"Henceforth be earls…"	
"calling home our exil'd friends abroad"	
"what needful else/…by the grace of Grace/We will perform"	

e) This last speech would no doubt have prompted reflections by the audience of Shakespeare's day. What might the speech cause them to think about and relate to in their own situation?

Upgrade

No work of art exists in a vacuum. The best are influenced by the context in which they were written, and in turn influence what is yet to come. Contextual factors are important in *Macbeth* and should find their way into your analysis whenever it is appropriate.

Progress check

Use the chart below to review the skills you have developed in this chapter. For each column, start at the bottom box and work your way up towards the highest level in the top box. Tick the box to show you have achieved that level.

I can sustain a critical response to *Macbeth* and interpret the context convincingly ☐	I can use well-integrated textual references from *Macbeth* to support my interpretation ☐	I can show a perceptive understanding of how *Macbeth* is shaped by its context ☐
I can develop a coherent response to *Macbeth* and explain the context clearly ☐	I can use quotations and other textual references from *Macbeth* to support my explanation ☐	I understand the context of *Macbeth* and can make connections between the text and its context ☐
I can make some comments on the context in *Macbeth* ☐	I can make references to some details from *Macbeth* ☐	I am aware of the context in which *Macbeth* was written ☐
Personal response	**Textual references**	**Text and context**

23

Characters

Macbeth

We hear about Macbeth before we actually meet him in the play.

Activity 1

Reread Act 1 Scene 2.

a) Pick out four adjectives that are used to describe Macbeth in this scene.

----

b) What overall impression does this scene give of Macbeth?

Activity 2

a) In Macbeth's first encounter with the witches in Act 1 Scene 3, another aspect of his character is revealed. What is it and how do we know?

----

b) Sum up what we learn about Macbeth's thinking at this early stage in the play. Refer to the quotations below in your answer.

"Two truths are told,
As happy prologues to the swelling act
Of the imperial theme."

(Act 1, Scene 3)

"If chance will have me king, why chance
may crown me
Without my stir."

(Act 1, Scene 3)

Activity 3

At the beginning of Act 1 Scene 5, Lady Macbeth reads a letter. Her thinking about what it says reveals further aspects of Macbeth's character. Fill in the table below, quoting Lady Macbeth's lines to support the character **traits** identified.

Macbeth's character trait	Quotation
Kindness	
Ambition	
Weakness	
Honesty	

Activity 4

At the beginning of Act 1 Scene 7 we hear Macbeth's first **soliloquy**. This gives us a detailed insight into his thinking at this stage of the play, and also reveals a good deal about his character.

Add three further aspects of Macbeth's character that you learn from this speech to the table below.

Macbeth's character trait	Quotation

soliloquy where a character voices aloud their innermost thoughts for the audience to hear

trait a person's distinguishing quality or characteristic

Activity 5

At the end of Act 1 Scene 7, Macbeth says:

"I am settled and bend up
Each corporal agent to this terrible feat.

[…]

False face must hide what the false heart doth know."

What has happened to change Macbeth's mind? Look carefully at what Lady Macbeth says in the second half of the scene.

Activity 6

Complete the spider diagram below to show what impression the audience has of Macbeth at the end of Act 1. Use your answers to Activities 1 to 5 above.

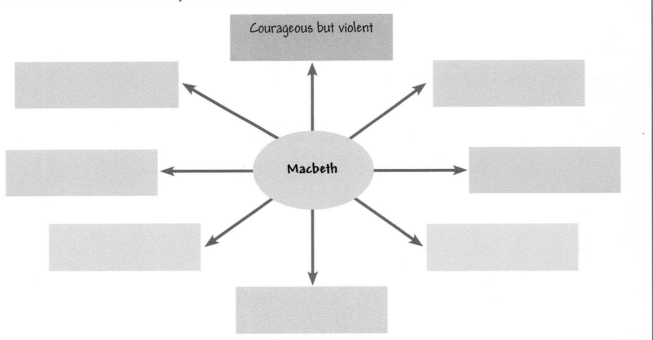

Courageous but violent

Macbeth

Upgrade

Notice how the emphasis in the activities on pages 26 and 27 is on Shakespeare's *presentation* of the character of Macbeth. You will always be asked about how the playwright presents (crafts) the character, not simply what the character does.

One of the most interesting facets of Shakespeare's presentation of Macbeth is that we are allowed to see his mental state through the course of the play rather than simply his actions.

Activity 7

a) Here are five reasons why Shakespeare might have revealed Macbeth's mental state. Put a tick by those that you think are true.

A story consisting only of action, suspense and horror would bore the audience.

Knowing Macbeth's inner thoughts allows the audience to feel more sympathetic towards him.

'Thinking space' comes as light relief from the endless violence.

Shakespeare was interested in human triumphs and failings, and the reasons for them.

As the main character, Macbeth is fully rounded. Without access to his thinking he would come across as more of a straightforward villain.

b) Which one of these reasons do you feel is the most important? Why do you think so?

----

c) There are two occasions in the play where Macbeth seems to suffer from hallucinations. What are they?

----

d) These hallucinations seem to be brought on by Macbeth's conscience. What insights do they give us into his character?

----

e) Does Macbeth always fully believe in the witches and what they tell him? On a separate piece of paper, copy and complete the table below and find evidence (for and against) to answer this question.

Does Macbeth always believe in what the witches tell him?	
Yes: evidence	**No: evidence**

Activity 8

As Macbeth becomes a hardened and callous murderer, his outlook on life begins to change. Towards the end of the play it could be described as **nihilistic**.

Below is Macbeth's speech in Act 5 Scene 5 immediately after he has been told that his wife is dead. Annotate it to show what it reveals about Macbeth's state of mind and his view of life.

> Tomorrow, and tomorrow, and tomorrow
> **Creeps in this petty pace** from day to day
> To the last syllable of recorded time;
> And all our yesterdays have lighted fools
> The way to dusty death. Out, out, brief candle,
> Life's but a walking shadow, a poor player
> That struts and frets his hour upon the stage
> And then is heard no more. It is a tale
> Told by an idiot, full of sound and fury
> Signifying nothing.

the days drag; they are unimportant

It would be easy to see Macbeth as a man who is easily persuaded, over-ambitious and increasingly brutal until he is killed and order is restored. However, this would be too simple a view. Because Macbeth is a complex character, Shakespeare can allow the audience some sympathy for him at the end of the play even after he has ordered the slaughter of innocent people.

nihilism believing that life is meaningless; refusing to believe in any moral principles

Activity 9

Note down four ways in which Macbeth engages our sympathy in the final section of the play (from Act 5 Scene 3 to the end) by completing the table below. Provide a quotation in each case. The first row is done for you.

We feel sympathy for Macbeth because...	Quotation
His allies desert him, leaving him to face overwhelming odds, but he refuses to give in.	"the heart I bear/Shall never sag with doubt nor shake with fear"

Activity 10

What can you infer about Macbeth from his lines at the end of Act 5 Scene 5?

"Blow wind, come wrack;
At least we'll die with harness on our back."

As noted in Chapter 1, the play begins and ends on a battlefield. In some ways, the Macbeth we see at the end is very different from the character who fought the Norwegians on behalf of his king, yet in some ways his character remains the same.

Activity 11

a) The boxes below list some of Macbeth's character traits. Fill in the blanks with other traits. Think about which of these qualities seem to remain constant through the play, and which of them change.

| courageous | ambitious | deceitful | easily persuaded |

| conscience-stricken | | | |

b) Sum up the changes in Macbeth's character, stating who or what brings them about.

Lady Macbeth

When we first meet Lady Macbeth, Shakespeare leaves us in no doubt about her ruthlessness, her desire to manipulate others and her lack of human feeling.
In Act 1 Scene 5 she says: *"And fill me from the crown to the toe topfull/ Of direst cruelty"*.

Activity 12

Choose two further quotations from Act 1 Scene 5 that make it clear to the audience what they are to think of Lady Macbeth at this point in the play. What does each quotation show about her character?

a) --

b) --

In Acts 1 to 3 Lady Macbeth seeks to help Macbeth in as many ways as she can. But where does help become control and manipulation?

Activity 13

a) Fill in the table below. Some examples have been given to start you off.

How Lady Macbeth helps Macbeth	Help or control? Give reasons
Act 2 Scene 2: She makes sure the plot goes according to plan.	
Act 3 Scene 4: She pretends to faint at the banquet to divert attention from him.	

b) What does all the evidence you have noted tell you about Lady Macbeth's character, and about her relationship with Macbeth?

In Act 3 Scene 4 Lady Macbeth tries to control a situation that is getting out of hand. Macbeth is behaving very strangely and is on the verge of revealing his responsibility for Banquo's murder.

Activity 14

What do the following quotations say about Lady Macbeth in this scene?

Lady Macbeth	What this shows
"My lord is often thus,/And hath been from his youth."	
"If much you note him/You shall offend him and extend his passion."	
"What, quite unmann'd in folly?"	
"Think of this, good peers,/But as a thing of custom. 'Tis no other,"	
"At once, good night./Stand not upon the order of your going,/But go at once."	

Act 3 Scene 4 is the last time that we see Lady Macbeth in her right mind.

Activity 15

a) What is the main thing that causes Lady Macbeth to become mentally unstable?

----

b) Annotate these Lady Macbeth lines in Act 5 Scene 1 to show how her feelings of guilt have overwhelmed her, and how her outlook has changed from earlier in the play.

> She imagines a spot of blood on her hand, despite vigorous attempts to clean it off. Compare with "A little water clears us of this deed" in Act 2 Scene 2.

Out, damned spot! Out, I say! One, two. Why then 'tis time to do't. Hell is murky. Fie, my lord, fie, a soldier, and afeard? What need we fear who knows it, when none can call our power to account? Yet who would have thought the old man to have had so much blood in him?

[…]

The Thane of Fife had a wife. Where is she now? What, will these hands ne'er be clean? No more o'that, my lord, no more o'that. You mar all with this starting.

c) Is it possible to feel sympathy for Lady Macbeth at this point? Some might say she simply gets what she deserves, whereas others may pity her final broken and distressed state. What do you think? Remember to justify your views.

Like Macbeth, Lady Macbeth is a complex character. Part of Shakespeare's great skill as a playwright is to present rounded, believably human characters.

Activity 16

Write a paragraph, complete with evidence in the form of quotation and/or reference, to summarize the development of Lady Macbeth's character across the play as a whole.

Upgrade

Lady Macbeth is often used as a byword for evil. When writing about her, it is easy to stress her diabolical features, but a more subtle analysis will take into account the ways that Shakespeare invites some sympathy for her, through both language and action.

Banquo

Banquo and Macbeth are equals at the beginning of the play. They are travelling together when they meet the witches. Both receive prophecies, but their reactions to them are very different. Banquo warns his friend against "the instruments of darkness" in Act 1 Scene 3.

Key quotation

But 'tis strange,

And oftentimes, to win us to our harm,

The instruments of darkness tell us truths;

Win us with honest trifles, to betray's

In deepest consequence.

(Act 1 Scene 3)

Activity 17

a) What is Banquo warning against in Act 1 Scene 3?

----

b) How does his warning come true?

----

c) What does his reaction to the witches tell us about his character at this early stage of the play?

Upgrade

Banquo makes few appearances in the play, but his effect is far-reaching. Bear in mind that for Shakespeare characters frequently serve a **function** or **symbolic purpose** in the play, as well as advancing the plot. It is always a good idea to write about what function the character might have if this is appropriate.

function (of character) the part a character plays in moving along the plot or highlighting a particular theme or themes

irony a literary technique where the intended meaning differs from what is said or presented directly

symbolic purpose the use of a character or object to represent a quality or theme (for example, goodness or truth)

Act 3 Scene 1 demonstrates very well Shakespeare's skill in characterization. By the end of the scene our earlier impressions of Banquo have been confirmed and we have learned more about Macbeth's increasing ruthlessness.

Activity 18

a) List briefly what happens in Act 3 Scene 1. The first event has been done for you.

i. Banquo expresses his doubts about Macbeth and his thoughts about the witches' prophecies.

ii. --

iii. --

iv. --

v. --

b) In the same scene, Macbeth provides a summary of Banquo's character just before
the murderers enter. How does he characterize Banquo?

----

c) Macbeth instructs Banquo: **"Fail not our feast"**, to which Banquo replies:
"My lord, I will not". How does this turn out to be an example of **irony**?

Activity 19

It has been said that Banquo represents everything good in order to highlight
everything that is bad about Macbeth. To find evidence for this contrast, complete the
table below.

Good in Banquo	Bad in Macbeth

Macduff

As the leader of the rebellion that eventually overthrows Macbeth, Macduff has a relatively small role. However, he is a significant character.

 Activity 20

a) In Act 4 Scene 2, Ross describes Macduff as **"noble, wise, judicious"**. Go through the play and find examples of what Macduff does or says to match such a description.

'noble' <

_____

_____

_____

'wise' <

_____

_____

'judicious' <

_____

_____

b) We see a little of Macduff's family in Act 4 Scene 2. What does this scene add to our understanding of Macduff himself?

_____

_____

_____

_____

_____

_____

_____

Activity 21

At a decisive moment in the plot, we find out that Macduff was born by caesarian section.

a) Quote the line that tells us (and Macbeth) this fact.

----

b) Why does this matter?

Macduff faces Macbeth in single combat. At this point we could say that he represents good fighting against evil, the hope of a better Scotland against the despair of continuing rule by a tyrant.

Activity 22

a) Here are some possible reasons for Macduff wanting to fight and kill Macbeth by himself alone. Put them in rank order, from the most important reason (1) to the least important (5).

He wants to show his prowess in single combat. ☐

He does not want any more of the rebel army to be killed. ☐

He is less concerned about himself and more concerned about restoring Scotland to King Malcolm. ☐

He stands to gain high position under the new king if he defeats Macbeth. ☐

He is burning for revenge against the man who ordered his family to be slaughtered. ☐

b) Why do you believe your top reason is the most important? Remember to support your view with evidence from the play.

Four kings

In the course of the play we see or hear of four kings: Duncan, Macbeth, Edward the Confessor and Malcolm.

Activity 23

Duncan is shown to be a good and gracious king. Everything he does shows nobility and generosity.

a) Find five examples in Act 1 of what Duncan says or does that show us that he is in many ways an ideal king.

i. _____

_____

ii. _____

_____

iii. _____

_____

iv. _____

_____

v. _____

_____

b) Characters are often developed by what others say about them. What do you learn of Duncan from Macbeth's first speech in Act 1 Scene 7?

_____

_____

_____

_____

The counterbalancing of good and bad kingship in the play can be explored through comparing the words and deeds of the rightful kings and the **usurper**.

usurper someone who seizes the crown without the right to do so

Activity 24

Fill in the table below. For each of Macbeth's evil thoughts or deeds in the course of the play, find one or more actions by the remaining kings that present the opposite qualities. The first one is given as an example.

Macbeth	Duncan, Malcolm, Edward
Following the witches' first prophecies, begins to think about being king.	Following the opening battle, Duncan thinks of rewarding those who have served him faithfully.

⊕ Progress check

Use the chart below to review the skills you have developed in this chapter. For each column, start at the bottom box and work your way up towards the highest level in the top box. Tick the box to show you have achieved that level.

I can sustain a critical response to *Macbeth* and interpret the characterization convincingly ☐	I can use well-integrated textual references from *Macbeth* to support my interpretation ☐
I can develop a coherent response to *Macbeth* and explain the characterization clearly ☐	I can use quotations and other textual references from *Macbeth* to support my explanation ☐
I can make some comments on the characterization in *Macbeth* ☐	I can make references to some details from *Macbeth* ☐
Personal response	**Textual references**

Verse and prose

prose any writing in continuous form without rhythm or rhyme

verse a group or series of groups of written lines, containing a rhythm or rhyme

It is important to remember that Shakespeare, like all playwrights, wrote words to be heard, not read. In Shakespeare's time, very few people could read, and in any case, plays were rarely printed because the acting companies were afraid that the scripts would be pirated and performed by their rivals. Shakespeare's audiences were very used to listening carefully. They delighted in wordplay, puns, alliteration, striking visual images and shifts in pace and tone.

There were certain conventions in the way characters spoke on stage in Shakespeare's time. The use of **prose** and **verse** is one way of presenting different kinds of characters.

Activity 1

a) Look at these two speeches. Annotate which features identify Extract A as verse and Extract B as prose.

Extract A

> Methought I heard a voice cry, 'Sleep no more:
>
> Macbeth does murder sleep', the innocent sleep,
>
> Sleep that knits up the ravell'd sleeve of care,
>
> The death of each day's life, sore labour's bath…
>
> *(Act 2 Scene 2)*

Extract B

> Here's a knocking indeed: if a man were porter of hell-gate, he should have old turning the key. Knock, knock, knock. Who's there i'th'name of Beelzebub? Here's a farmer that hanged himself on th'expectation of plenty.
>
> *(Act 2 Scene 3)*

b) Who speaks the extracts opposite?

Extract A ---

Extract B ---

c) Note down the names of three other characters who speak in verse and find a quotation in the text.

i. ---

----

ii. --

----

iii. ---

----

d) Note down two other characters who speak in prose and find a quotation in the text.

i. ---

----

ii. --

----

e) What would you say is the main difference between those who use verse and those who speak in prose?

A further convention in Shakespeare's time was that the verse spoken should be in **iambic pentameter** form. This particular rhythm made conversation sound a little more natural, and was very flexible in terms of what could be achieved with it.

> **iambic pentameter** a line of verse with ten syllables, where the stress falls on the second syllable (and then every other syllable) in the line

Activity 2

Here are two lines from Act 5 Scene 9, annotated to show the iambic pentameter rhythm by adding a forward slash above the stressed syllables.

>   /   /   /   /   /
> So, thanks to all at once and to each one,
>   /   /   /   /   /
> whom we invite to see us crown'd at scone.

Notice how full stops and commas help the sense of the line but do not disturb the rhythm.

a) The following lines come from Act 1 Scene 7. Annotate them for their rhythm by marking the stressed syllables in each line, as in the example above.

> And pity, like a naked newborn babe
>
> Striding the blast, or heaven's cherubin hors'd
>
> Upon the sightless couriers of the air,
>
> Shall blow the horrid deed in every eye,
>
> That tears shall drown the wind. I have no spur

b) Now mark the stressed syllables in part of the witches' speech in Act 4 Scene 1.

> Fillet of a fenny snake,
>
> In the cauldron boil and bake:
>
> Eye of newt, and toe of frog,
>
> Wool of bat, and tongue of dog,
>
> Adder's fork, and blind-worm's sting,
>
> Lizard's leg, and howlet's wing,

c) What do you notice about the rhythm in the witches' speech above, in Activity 2b? In what ways is it different from Macbeth's speech in Activity 2a?

----

d) Look up the term 'trochaic tetrameter'. Write down the definition of this metrical form.

----

e) Shakespeare wrote the lines of the witches so that they sounded very different. Think of two dramatic or stagecraft reasons why he might do this.

You may have noticed in the activities above that the witches' lines rhyme, whereas Macbeth's do not. Iambic pentameter lines do not have to rhyme and in Shakespeare's later plays they rarely do; this is **blank verse**.

blank verse poetry that has iambic pentameter but does not rhyme

Activity 3

a) Look again at the witches' lines in Act 4 Scene 1. You will see that as well as having a fixed rhythm each pair of lines rhymes. What is the technical term for this sort of rhyme? (Hint: you may need to look up the word 'trochee'.)

----

b) Look at the last lines of Act 1 Scene 2, Act 2 Scene 1, Act 3 Scene 2 and Act 4 Scene 3. What do you notice about these lines?

----

c) Tick which of these reasons you would accept to explain the form of these lines.

Shakespeare forgot he was writing in iambic pentameter. ☐

It makes a change from the rest of the scene for the audience. ☐

It signals the end of a scene for the audience. ☐

This always happens before a character leaves the stage. ☐

It is accidental. ☐

Establishing setting and character

Language is also used to establish settings and characters. Remember that in Shakespeare's theatre there was very little in the way of scenery or props, and no lighting. (Plays were performed in the afternoon.) Without being told, therefore, the audience had no way of knowing where scenes were taking place, nor who the characters were. This presented a problem for the dramatist, who needed the audience to follow the plot and the characters carefully.

Activity 4

At the beginning of Act 1 Scene 6, the audience knows that the characters are approaching Macbeth's castle. Duncan says: **"This castle hath a pleasant seat; the air/Nimbly and sweetly recommends itself/Unto our gentle senses"**.

Act 2 Scene 1 sets the scene by letting the audience know that it is the early hours of the morning and pitch black (**"How goes the night, boy?" "The moon is down"**).

Find three further examples of 'scene setting' – in different locations – by what the characters say to each other.

a) _____

_____

b) _____

_____

c) _____

_____

Just as there was very little scenery available to Shakespeare, so costumes were also scarce. The witches might be dressed in rags, and the noble characters would have basic robes, but the dramatist needed to help the audience establish who the characters were.

Activity 5

At the beginning of Act 1 Scene 2, Malcolm tells the Captain: **"Say to the king the knowledge of the broil"**. This confirms for the audience that the central character in the scene is the king.

a) Following the exit of the Captain in Act 1 Scene 2, there is another example of 'character introduction'. What is it?

_____

_____

b) Find two further examples of characters being introduced through what other characters say.

_____

_____

Pace and tone

If characters simply stood on the stage and **declaimed** their lines, there would be no variety for the audience. Similarly, if all speeches used the same rhythms the audience might lose interest. Skilful dramatists knew how to avoid these problems by varying the pace and tone of the language.

> **declaim** to pronounce words loudly and clearly in a precisely articulated manner

Activity 6

Read these two extracts. On a separate piece of paper, note the differences between them in terms of tone and pace. (Both are in iambic pentameter, which may surprise you.)

Extract A

Macbeth	I have done the deed. Didst thou not hear a noise?
Lady Macbeth	I heard the owl scream and the crickets cry.
	Did not you speak?
Macbeth	When?
Lady Macbeth	Now.
Macbeth	As I descended?
Lady Macbeth	Ay.

(Act 2 Scene 2)

Extract B

Macbeth	Tomorrow, and tomorrow, and tomorrow
	Creeps in this petty pace from day to day
	To the last syllable of recorded time;
	And all our yesterdays have lighted fools
	The way to dusty death. Out, out, brief candle,
	Life's but a walking shadow, a poor player
	That struts and frets his hour upon the stage
	And then is heard no more. It is a tale
	Told by an idiot, full of sound and fury
	Signifying nothing.

(Act 5 Scene 5)

Wordplay

In Act 2 Scene 3, Macbeth says: **"Here lay Duncan,/His silver skin lac'd with his golden blood"**. There is an interesting use of the idea of precious metals here, and the contrast between gold and silver, but in fact the idea of **'golden blood'** has been planted earlier. In Act 2 Scene 2, Lady Macbeth says: **"If he do bleed,/I'll gild the faces of the grooms withal,/For it must seem their guilt"**.

'Gild' means 'to coat with gold', and if something is 'gilt' it has a golden sheen to it, but of course 'gilt' sounds exactly like **'guilt'**, which has an entirely different meaning. Lady Macbeth is making a grim **pun**.

Shakespeare's audience delighted in wordplay of this sort. They had a keen ear for skill with language, and there are countless examples in *Macbeth*.

> **ambiguity** using words or phrases where the meaning is not clear, and where something can be interpreted in different ways
>
> **pun** using the different meanings of words, or their similar sounds, to create an effect, often humorous but sometimes startling

 Activity 7

a) Explain the wordplay that is happening in the following quotations by annotating the key words and explaining their possible meanings (as with 'gilt' and 'guilt' above).

i. Banquo is murdered and Fleance escapes (Act 3 Scene 3)

> **Third murderer**   Who did strike out the light?

ii. Donaldbain (Act 2 Scene 3)

> There's daggers in men's smiles; the nea'er in blood,
> The nearer bloody.

iii. Doctor (Act 5 Scene 1)

> Well, well, well—

b) Find three further examples of Shakespeare's skill in wordplay.

- -

- -

- -

- -

- -

- -

- -

c) What do you think the use of wordplay contributes to the experience of watching the play? Put the following answers in rank order where (1) is the most important reason and (5) is the least important.

The audience would smile at a pun, bringing much-needed relief from the slaughter they were seeing on the stage.

- - - - - - -

The audience went to the theatre to listen out for wordplay. They were less interested in the story.

- - - - - - -

Plays had to have wordplay in them or they would not be successful.

- - - - - - -

Wordplay was part of the experience of theatre; it was expected by audiences.

- - - - - - -

Wordplay was one of the ways in which a playwright was judged. The better the wordplay, the more skilful the playwright.

- - - - - - -

Ambiguity and irony

Both **ambiguity** and irony are aspects of wordplay, and both are prominent in the play. Indeed, the ambiguity in the witches' prophecies could be said to drive the plot.

Activity 8

In Act 5 Scene 8 Macbeth says:

"And be these juggling fiends no more believ'd

That palter* with us in a double sense,

That keep the word of promise to our ear

And break it to our hope."

***palter**: trifle with

What idea is Macbeth expressing here? How does the language of this speech emphasize deliberate ambiguity?

Ambiguity depends on different possible meanings. In the play, Macbeth interprets the prophecies in one way when (as it turns out) the witches had a different meaning in mind.

 Activity 9

a) Complete the table below. For each of the ambiguous prophecies of the witches in Act 4 write down what Macbeth took it to mean and what the witches meant.

Prophecy	Macbeth's meaning	Witches' meaning
"...none of woman born/Shall harm Macbeth."		
"Macbeth shall never vanquish'd be until/Great Birnam Wood to high Dunsinane Hill/Shall come against him."		

b) Focus on the exact word or words where the ambiguity lies. Explain the possible meanings of these words in the prophecies listed above.

"...none of woman born/Shall harm Macbeth."

"Macbeth shall never vanquish'd be until/Great Birnam Wood to high Dunsinane Hill/Shall come against him."

Upgrade

When writing about ambiguity and irony in the play, it will not be enough just to give examples. You need to explain what the ambiguity and the irony *add* to the play. They should be linked to the idea of equivocation that runs through the play.

Activity 10

In Act 3 Scene 1 there is an interchange between Macbeth and Banquo:

Macbeth	Fail not our feast.
Banquo	My lord, I will not.

Of course, since Macbeth is about to have Banquo murdered, he knows that Banquo will not make it to the feast – yet he does.

a) How?

This is a good example of irony.

b) Explain the irony in the lines below.

   i. Duncan, referring to the Thane of Cawdor, who has been executed for treason (Act 1 Scene 4):

There's no art
To find the mind's construction in the face.
He was a gentleman on whom I built
An absolute trust.

----

ii. Lady Macbeth (Act 2 Scene 2):

> These deeds must not be thought
> After these ways; so, it will make us mad.

----

iii. Lady Macbeth (Act 2 Scene 2):

> A little water clears us of this deed.

Imagery

In Shakespeare's time, poetry relied to some extent on making striking visual **imagery**. It was also part of the experience of hearing a play: the audience expected to be presented with images that would allow them to see things in new or different ways and to deepen their understanding of characters and events.

figurative language language that uses figures of speech, is **metaphorical** and not literal

imagery visually descriptive or **figurative language**

metaphor the use of a word or phrase in a way that is not literal, for example, Duncan's planting and nurturing metaphor in Act 1 Scene 4

simile a comparison of one thing with another, using 'as' or 'like', for example, "signs of nobleness like stars shall shine" *(Act 1 Scene 4)*

Activity 11

Simple images often use **similes**. To explain a simile, we need to state what two things are being compared and in what ways they are similar. This will often reveal an interesting or novel aspect of a character or an action.

Complete the following table. Find five similes from the play, and for each one explain what is compared and how the comparison works. One is given as an example.

Simile	What is compared?	How does the comparison work?
"Their drenched natures lies as in a death" (Act 1 Scene 7)	The drugged grooms on the floor, so still that they might be dead.	The depth of their drunken sleep is emphasized through a comparison with lying dead (which they soon will be).

Metaphor is a more complex form of figurative language, but like simile it is used to add depth to an image and to help the audience to understand an idea or a character better. Shakespeare's writing is often highly metaphorical. For example, Duncan says to Macbeth: *"I have begun to plant thee and will labour/To make thee full of growing"* *(Act 1 Scene 4)*.

The comparison here is between Macbeth and a young plant. Duncan promises to work hard to make sure that the plant grows. There is no sense in which we should read this literally – clearly Macbeth is not a seedling – but it neatly highlights for us the idea of Duncan as a nurturing and generous king.

Activity 12

a) As you did with the similes, find five metaphors from different scenes in the play. On a separate piece of paper, explain what is being compared and how the comparison works.

b) Now take this one stage further. For each of the metaphors you have chosen, state what the comparison adds to our understanding of character or action.

Metaphor	What does it add?
1	
2	
3	
4	
5	

Image and motif

In *Macbeth*, particular images often recur. For example, there are over 40 uses of the word 'blood'. Blood is clearly a **motif** and complements several of the themes of the play. Other motifs include murder, fate, fortune and chance.

> **motif** a word, phrase or image in literature that is repeated to create specific effects. Note that this is slightly different from a recurring *image*, where different words may be used to evoke the same word picture.

Upgrade

When writing about language in the play, remember that it is not enough simply to 'spot' the features or devices covered in this chapter. You must always go on to say what the effect of the feature might be on the audience.

Activity 13

To explore Shakespeare's use of motifs in the language of the play, complete the following spider diagram. Add an act, scene and line reference after the phrase. This will help you to see how a motif is spread across the play.

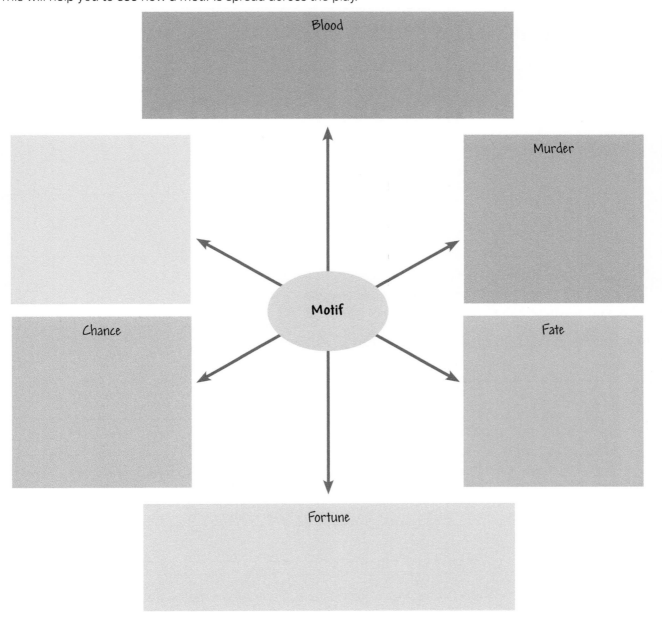

Blood

Murder

Chance

Motif

Fate

Fortune

Imagery and image patterns

In *Macbeth* several images recur often. In this way they form a pattern or thread running through the play.

One of the most prominent image threads concerns clothing. The play explores the idea of masking someone's true nature or revealing some aspect of the inner personality through references to clothing.

Activity 14

a) Look through the scenes given in the table below to find references to clothing. An example has been done for you.

Scene	Quotation
Act 1 Scene 3	Macbeth: "Why do you dress me/In borrow'd robes?"
Act 1 Scene 3 (a different clothing image)	
Act 1 Scene 7	
Act 2 Scene 4	
Act 5 Scene 2	

A further set of images relates to children, infants and babies, along with the idea of children inheriting from their parents. For example, Macbeth refers to pity as a **"naked newborn babe"** *(Act 1 Scene 7)*.

b) What other examples of images of 'children' can you find in the play?

---

c) What is the effect of the play's focus on very young children?

---

d) Act 3 Scene 4 is 'the banquet scene', so there are naturally many images connected with feasting. Find three references to feasting in Act 3 Scene 4, and a further three in the rest of the play.

----

e) What might Shakespeare be using recurring feasting images to suggest?

----

f) Write two paragraphs in which you explore image patterns in the play. Give examples from different groups of images (including examples other than those you have already used in this activity) and explain the purpose of this patterning in the language of the play as a whole. Write your paragraphs on separate paper.

 # Progress check

Use the chart below to review the skills you have developed in this chapter. For each column, start at the bottom box and work your way up towards the highest level in the top box. Tick the box to show you have achieved that level.

I can sustain a critical response to *Macbeth* and interpret the language convincingly ☐	I can use well-integrated textual references from *Macbeth* to support my interpretation ☐	I can analyse the effects of Shakespeare's use of language, structure and form in *Macbeth*, using subject terms judiciously ☐	I use a wide range of vocabulary and can spell and punctuate consistently accurately ☐
I can develop a coherent response to *Macbeth* and explain the language clearly ☐	I can use quotations and other textual references from *Macbeth* to support my explanation ☐	I can explain how Shakespeare uses language, structure and form to create effects in *Macbeth*, using relevant subject terms ☐	I use a range of vocabulary and can spell and punctuate, mostly accurately ☐
I can make some comments on the language in *Macbeth* ☐	I can make references to some details from *Macbeth* ☐	I can identify some of Shakespeare's methods in *Macbeth* and use some subject terms ☐	I use a simple range of vocabulary and spell and punctuate with some accuracy ☐
Personal response	**Textual references**	**Language, structure, form**	**Technical accuracy**

Themes

Themes in the play

Macbeth has a number of **themes**. We have already mentioned equivocation and ambiguity, but there are other ideas that run through the play. The themes are expressed through language, which uses different ways of referring to the same or similar ideas.

> **theme** a significant idea that recurs in a poem, play or novel

Activity 1

a) Which of the following themes are present in *Macbeth*? Circle those that you can clearly identify.

feasting

dress/clothing

kingship

exploration

infants/babies

witchcraft/superstition

ambition

teaching

love

honour

b) Choose two of the themes you have identified. For each theme, give at least three quotations to show how the theme recurs in the play. Ideally, the quotations you choose should be from different characters.

Theme 1:

Theme 2:

Good and evil

The main theme in *Macbeth* is perhaps the exploration of the nature of good and evil. Many of the major characters seem to have both qualities.

Activity 2

Complete the following table by giving examples of the good that the characters display in their deeds or thoughts and the evil that they show. Note that for some characters you may need to leave one of the boxes empty.

Character	Examples of good	Examples of evil
Macbeth		
Lady Macbeth		
Banquo		
Duncan		
Macduff		
Witches		

Activity 3

In Act 1 Scene 1 the witches chant: **"Fair is foul, and foul is fair"**. Macbeth's first line in the play (Act 1 Scene 3) is: **"So foul and fair a day I have not seen"**.

Find three examples of behaviour by a character or characters that seems **'fair'** but masks something **'foul'**.

- ---

- ---

- ---

Activity 4

In Act 4 Scene 2 Lady Macduff says: **"I am in this earthly world where to do harm/Is often laudable, to do good sometime/Accounted dangerous folly"**.

Find three examples in the play where **'to do harm'** is seen as **'laudable'** or **'to do good'** is seen as **'dangerous folly'**.

- _____
  _____

- _____
  _____

- _____
  _____

Activity 5

a) What ideas about good and evil do you think Shakespeare was presenting in the play? Place the following in rank order from most important (1) to least important (5).

Good has no chance when it is confronted by overwhelming evil. [_____]

Most people have both good and bad in them. [_____]

Goodness can be tempted into committing evil deeds. [_____]

Good will always triumph over evil. [_____]

External forces are responsible for the evil in the world; people are not naturally bad. [_____]

b) What evidence can you find in the play to support your choice of its most important idea?

_____

_____

_____

_____

Activity 6

a) Plot the 'good/evil' graph below to show how good and evil develop in the play. For each scene identified, plot a point showing whether good is displayed or whether there is evil. (Take the first entrance of the witches as 'neutral' – that is, at the midpoint – since we cannot tell at the outset how to interpret it.) The height or depth of the point should relate to how good or how evil you believe the actions to be. Once you have plotted the points, draw lines between them.

Good

Evil

First entrance of witches

Macbeth brave in battle

Macbeth rewarded for courage

Lady Macbeth reads letter

Macbeth murders Duncan

Murder of Banquo

Witches' second prophecy

Macduff's family murdered

Lady Macbeth sleepwalks

Malcolm's army marches to Dunsinane

Malcolm's army begins battle

Macduff kills Macbeth

b) Describe in one paragraph what the graph shows you about the interplay of good and evil in the play.

Kingship

When *Macbeth* was first performed, James I was relatively new to the throne of England. There is some evidence to show that the play was specially written by Shakespeare as an entertainment for the king, who in 1606 was hosting a visit by King Christian of Denmark. It is not surprising, then, that one of the play's themes is the nature of kingship.

Activity 7

a) Write down the names of all the kings we see (or hear of) in the course of the play.

_____

b) Reread the beginning of Act 1 Scene 7. We are told that Duncan **"Hath borne his faculties so meek"** and that he **"hath been/So clear in his great office"**. Explain why these lines present an ideal summing up of a good king.

_____

_____

_____

c) In Act 4 Scene 3 Malcolm describes the type of character that a good king must have. Annotate the speech by finding a different word that means the same or nearly the same as each of the qualities that Malcolm lists.

fairness →

> The king-becoming graces—
>
> As justice, verity, temp'rance, stableness,
>
> Bounty, perseverance, mercy, lowliness,
>
> Devotion, patience, courage, fortitude—

d) Which characters in the play display some or all of these characteristics? List them in the table below and support your views with evidence from the text.

Character	Qualities	Evidence
Macduff	Courage	He meets Macbeth in single combat, prepared to give everything for his cause.

Activity 8

a) Who is the king referred to in the speech beginning: **"'Tis called the Evil"** *(Act 4 Scene 3)*?

----

b) List the kingly qualities that this speech describes.

----

c) How do these qualities add to the idea of a good king?

----

d) Later in the same scene, Ross describes the terrible state of Scotland with Macbeth as its king, including the lines: **"The deadman's knell/Is there scarce ask'd for who, and good men's lives/Expire before the flowers in their caps"**.

Starting with this speech, and drawing further evidence from the play as a whole, how would you describe Macbeth's kingship?

Manhood

Related to the exploration of kingship in the play is the notion of manhood. Running under the action is a discussion of what exactly it is to be a man.

Activity 9

a) In Act 1 Scene 7, what qualities of a man does Lady Macbeth accuse her husband of lacking?

_____

_____

_____

b) In Act 3 Scene 4, when Macbeth sees the ghost of Banquo, he once again fails to live up to this idea of what 'manliness' is. Lady Macbeth asks him: **"What, quite unmann'd in folly?"** What is Macbeth's response?

_____

Activity 10

The view of manhood put forward by Lady Macbeth and seemingly shared by her husband is contrasted with those of other characters.

In Act 4 Scene 3, when Ross brings the news of the murder of Lady Macduff and her children, Malcolm tells Macduff to **"Dispute it like a man"**. In what ways does Macduff's response give a subtly different view of what it is to be a man?

_____

_____

_____

Activity 11

'In Shakespeare's view Lady Macbeth is more like a man and Lady Macduff is more of an ideal woman.'

Find evidence to support this view. Look particularly at Act 1 Scene 5, Act 1 Scene 7 and Act 4 Scene 2.

_____

_____

_____

_____

_____

Appearance and reality

We have already looked at the early line in the play: *"Fair is foul, and foul is fair"* *(Act 1 Scene 1)*. This introduces the play's central theme of good and evil, but it also hints at another theme: appearance and reality. If things are often the opposite of what they seem, then life becomes very difficult.

Activity 12

a) How can a day be both **'foul'** and **'fair'** at the same time? Explain Macbeth's opening line: **"So foul and fair a day I have not seen"** *(Act 1 Scene 3)*. In what ways is the day foul and in what ways fair?

_____

_____

_____

b) The witches' prophecies appear **'fair'** to Macbeth, but in reality are **'foul'**. Explain how this can be so.

_____

_____

_____

Activity 13

In Act 1 Scene 4 Duncan says: **"There's no art/To find the mind's construction in the face"**. He is referring to the Thane of Cawdor, who has betrayed him, but this idea runs through the whole play.

Find two further examples of where a **'face'** masks what is in the mind. Look particularly at Act 1 Scene 6 and the first part of Act 3 Scene 1.

- _____

_____

_____

_____

- _____

_____

_____

_____

Activity 14

The theme of appearance and reality is perhaps most clearly seen in the character of Lady Macbeth. At many points in the play she gives a false appearance, or attempts to disguise or draw attention away from the reality of the situation.

On a separate piece of paper, draw up a table like the one below, giving examples of this behaviour. For each example, find a quotation from Lady Macbeth that supports the idea of the appearance not being the reality, and comment on how the quotation hints at this. The first row is completed for you.

Appearance (surface speech or action) / reality (actual thought or intention)	Quotation	Comment
Welcomes Duncan (Act I Scene 6) BUT has arranged for Macbeth to murder him	"... those honours deep and broad wherewith/Your majesty loads our house"	The honours appear to be the king's visit, but actually will be the honour of kingship itself, which Macbeth seizes.

Chaos, natural order and the supernatural

In Shakespeare's time, there was an overwhelming belief in the natural order of all things. This belief was based on what was known as the Great Chain of Being.

Activity 15

a) Research the Great Chain of Being. In the space below, write out the order in which people in Shakespeare's time thought that everything in heaven and earth was organized.

> Highest   God
>
>
>
>
>
>
>
> Lowest

b) Within this chain, humans were further ranked. Who was at the top of the chain? Who was at the bottom?

- -

Any disturbance in the natural order was considered **ominous**.

ominous a warning sign that something bad might happen

Activity 16

a) Reread Lennox's speech early in Act 2 Scene 3 (just before the discovery of the king's murder). What disturbances in nature does Lennox report?

----

b) Why does Shakespeare place this speech at this point in the play? Tick the reasons that you think apply.

It's a dramatic device to delay the discovery of the murdered king. ☐

It's the sort of conversation people might have in the circumstances. ☐

A disruption in nature would be taken to be an omen by the audience: a sign of something terrible about to happen. ☐

It builds Lennox's part for the actor playing him. ☐   It's idle chat. ☐

It contrasts the inadequacy of Macbeth's response, showing that he (Macbeth) is distracted. ☐

65

Activity 17

a) Once the king is murdered, chaos ensues. Think back to the research you did on the Great Chain of Being, and explain why the killing of a king was seen as the most grievous disruption of the natural order.

----

b) Macbeth is an 'unnatural' king. List at least five chaotic consequences that follow in the rest of the play from his killing of Duncan.

We saw earlier that King James, who was on the throne when this play was written, was interested in the supernatural. The word 'supernatural' means above or beyond what is natural or normal, and clearly the play involves a large element of what Macbeth calls 'supernatural soliciting'. Bear in mind that people in Shakespeare's time believed that witchcraft was a reality and that witches were in league with the Devil.

Key quotation

This supernatural soliciting

Cannot be ill, cannot be good. If ill,

Why hath it given me earnest of success,

Commencing in a truth?

(Act 1 Scene 3)

Activity 18

a) Early in the play, the witches' prophecies come true. Macbeth says the key quotation on page 66.

What reason does Macbeth give for beginning to believe that this supernatural insight means good will come to him?

----

b) What is the answer to the question Macbeth asks in the quotation on page 66? (Think about what happens in the rest of the play.)

----

c) How important do you think witchcraft and the supernatural are in the play? Circle your choice.

vital   very important   one of several important themes   not important

Explain your choice, referring to events and themes in the play, and to the context in which it was first performed. (See Chapter 2 for information on context.) Support your ideas by referring closely to the text.

Writing about theme

Here is the opening paragraph of a student answer to the question 'How does Shakespeare present the theme of kingship in the play?' The paragraph has been annotated to indicate what it does reasonably well (yellow) and what is not so successful (purple).

A useful statement of a point of view. The rest of the paragraph should go on to explain why this is the case.

True, but rather vague. How many kings? What effect does their behaviour have on events and on the audience?

This idea needs much more explanation. Who do we only hear about? How does this add depth to the kingship theme?

This is an important point and needs developing.

Kingship is an important theme in the play. We see different kings and different ways they behave although in one case we only hear about him and what he does rather than seeing him. The obvious comparison Shakespeare makes is between Duncan and Macbeth as kings. This would have been a compliment to King James when he watched the play as he was Scottish where all the action took place.

An attempt to mention context, but very vague and unclear.

Not strictly true (Act 4 Scene 3 is in England), but the point is not well expressed and the connection between James, Scotland and kingship is not at all clear.

Activity 19

Write a detailed exploration of the theme of kingship in the play, bearing in mind the annotations above. Draw evidence from across the play and from relevant aspects of its context.

Upgrade

There is a big difference between *stating* a theme in the play with some supporting evidence and *exploring* a theme. Better answers will always suggest how the theme fits into the overall scheme of the play's themes and ideas, and how it shapes both the characters and the action. The best answers will also consider the interplay of theme, language and motif, ranging across the whole play for evidence to support points made.

Progress check

Use the chart below to review the skills you have developed in this chapter. For each column, start at the bottom box and work your way up towards the highest level in the top box. Tick the box to show you have achieved that level.

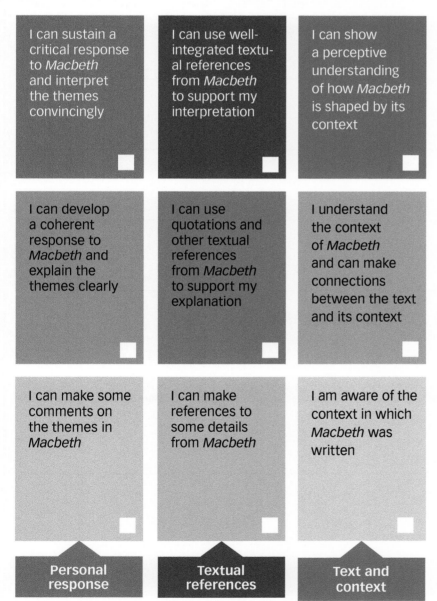

I can sustain a critical response to *Macbeth* and interpret the themes convincingly

I can use well-integrated textual references from *Macbeth* to support my interpretation

I can show a perceptive understanding of how *Macbeth* is shaped by its context

I can develop a coherent response to *Macbeth* and explain the themes clearly

I can use quotations and other textual references from *Macbeth* to support my explanation

I understand the context of *Macbeth* and can make connections between the text and its context

I can make some comments on the themes in *Macbeth*

I can make references to some details from *Macbeth*

I am aware of the context in which *Macbeth* was written

Personal response

Textual references

Text and context

Performance

As we noted in Chapter 1, Shakespeare's plays were written to be heard and seen, not to be read. *Macbeth* is one of his most frequently performed plays, and is probably in production somewhere in the world every single day.

Performance in Shakespeare's time

Activity 1

Shakespeare and his company performed in two different theatres in 1606 when Macbeth was first staged: the Globe Theatre and the Blackfriars Theatre.

a) Research these two theatres. Find out about their design and location, the look of their stages, the type of audiences that attended each and the different facilities that each offered to a dramatist. Set out your findings in the table below.

	The Globe	The Blackfriars Theatre
Design/location		
Stage		
Audience		
Facilities		

b) From what you have discovered about the two theatres, suggest how the following scenes from *Macbeth* could be presented differently according to which stage they were on.

Scene	At the Globe	At the Blackfriars Theatre
Act 1 Scene 1		
Act 3 Scene 4		
Act 5 Scene 1		

The text we have today is neatly divided into acts and scenes, but in performance, both now and in Shakespeare's time, the action was fluid, with one scene flowing into another and actors entering and speaking before the previous exit was complete.

Activity 2

a) It is possible to overlap the end of Act 1 Scene 4 with the beginning of Act 1 Scene 5. What would be the effect on the audience of this? (Think about tone, pace and language.)

----

b) Find examples of other 'scene pairs' (or perhaps more than two consecutive scenes) where this performance style could be used. In each case, explain why the two scenes could run on without pause, and what the effect of this might be.

Scenes	Reason for no pause	Effect on an audience

Activity 3

Shakespeare's theatres had very little in the way of scenery. Many modern productions choose to do away with scenery altogether. How do we know where the action is taking place?

a) Look at the beginning of Act 1 Scene 6. What clues are there to inform an audience where the scene is taking place?

----

b) Find five further examples in the play of spoken lines that tell us where we are or what time of day or night it is. Remember that these do not always have to be at the beginning of a scene.

----

c) Shakespeare very rarely indicated what props an actor would need. Go through the play and make a props list. Remember that often props are used sparingly. What props are essential?

----

d) Sometimes a key decision has to be made about a prop. In Act 2 Scene 1, Macbeth has a speech with the lines: **"Is this a dagger which I see before me"**. Should a real (prop) dagger be available here or not? Why?

In a performance, there is a variety in the pace. Some scenes may be leisurely, with detailed discussion or interchange between characters, whereas others will be rapid, perhaps breathless or action packed.

The pace is controlled by the dramatist. Shakespeare used a number of techniques to vary the pace and thus to keep his audiences engaged.

Lady Macbeth	My husband?
Macbeth	I have done the deed. Didst thou not hear a noise?
Lady Macbeth	I heard the owl scream and the crickets cry.
	Did not you speak?
Macbeth	When?
Lady Macbeth	Now.
Macbeth	As I descended?
Lady Macbeth	Ay.
Macbeth	Hark, who lies i'th'second chamber?
Lady Macbeth	Donaldbain.

Activity 4

Look at the above extract from Act 2 Scene 2.

a) This scene is written in iambic pentameter (see Chapter 4). Explain what Shakespeare is doing with the rhythm here.

----

b) What is the effect of this in terms of pace?

Activity 5

a) A further technique is to indicate to an actor how a line or lines might be said by deliberately missing out a beat (forcing a pause or complete stop).

In Act 3 Scene 1, Macbeth has a line in the middle of his pentameter speech that simply reads: **"Farewell"**. There is a very good reason for this. Suggest what it is.

----

b) On a separate sheet of paper, collect examples of this technique. For each example, explain why Shakespeare might have chosen to miss a beat or beats.

Shakespeare sometimes wrote 'Enter' followed by a name or list of names at the beginning of or during a scene. Sometimes he wrote 'Exit' or 'Exeunt' at suitable points in a scene, but he was not consistent about this.

Modern editions of the play generally have entrances and exits 'tidied up' by an editor, but who is on stage when is really a matter of interpretation by the director.

Activity 6

Consider the following scenes or points in the play. Who is on stage in your view? Who might be on stage in a different performance? What is the effect of this variation?

Point in the play	On stage	Alternative interpretation: who might or might not be on stage?	Effect of the different decisions
First part of Act 2 Scene 1			
Act 3 Scene 3			
Act 4 Scene 3			
The end of the play			

Performance today

Activity 7

Some scenes in the play can be staged in several different ways. Explain how you would present each of the following scenes. Think about who is on stage, scenery and props, entrances and exits. (You may wish to make sketches on separate sheets of paper of what the audience would see.)

a) Act 3 Scene 4

b) Act 4 Scene 1

c) Act 5 Scene 4

Activity 8

In putting on *Macbeth*, a director will encounter problems that must be solved. Choose two of the following problems that a director has to think about, and for each one explain the decisions you would make on a separate piece of paper. Bear in mind that you can choose to set the play in more or less any time and place (or even in no particular time or place).

a) How to present the witches

b) Is Banquo to be present in the banquet scene?

c) How to stage the parade of kings (Act 4 Scene 1)

d) How the play should end

One of the most important elements of a director's job is to work with the actors to suggest how they should say their lines and how they should move about the stage. Many directors make notes on the script once they have decided how lines and movements should work.

Activity 9

If you were working with the actor playing Macbeth, what directions (movement and voice) would you give him or her for Macbeth's famous speech in Act 2 Scene 1? Annotate the speech with your decisions.

Is this a dagger which I see before me,

The handle toward my hand? Come, let me clutch thee:

I have thee not, and yet I see thee still.

Art thou not, fatal vision, sensible

To feeling as to sight? Or art thou but

A dagger of the mind, a false creation,

Proceeding from the heat-oppressed brain?

I see thee yet, in form as palpable

As this which now I draw.

Thou marshall'st me the way that I was going,

And such an instrument I was to use.

[…]

Now o'er the one half-world

Nature seems dead, and wicked dreams abuse

The curtain'd sleep. Witchcraft celebrates

Pale Hecate's off'rings, and wither'd murder,

Alarum'd by his sentinel, the wolf,

Whose howl's his watch, thus with his stealthy pace,

[…]

A bell rings

I go, and it is done. The bell invites me.

Hear it not, Duncan, for it is a knell

That summons thee to heaven or to hell.   [*Exit*

Casting a play means that the director chooses both the look of the actors on stage and the way in which they perform. There are important decisions to be made if the director's interpretation of the play is to be fully realized.

Activity 10

If you were staging a modern version of *Macbeth* with a military setting, what would you be looking for in terms of actors? Complete the table below and in each case give the reasons for your answer.

Question	Your decision	Reason
What age is Macbeth? What age is King Duncan?		
What differences (in terms of look, voice, age, etc.), if any, would you want between Lady Macbeth and Lady Macduff?		
What type of actors would you choose to play the Witches?		

Progress check

Use the chart below to review the skills you have developed in this chapter. For each column, start at the bottom box and work your way up towards the highest level in the top box. Tick the box to show you have achieved that level.

I can sustain a critical response to *Macbeth* and interpret the performance aspects convincingly ☐	I can use wellintegrated textual references from *Macbeth* to support my interpretation ☐
I can develop a coherent response to *Macbeth* and explain the performance aspects clearly ☐	I can use quotations and other textual references from *Macbeth* to support my explanation ☐
I can make some comments on the performance aspects in *Macbeth* ☐	I can make references to some details from *Macbeth* ☐
Personal response	**Textual references**

Skills and Practice

Question types

An assessment question on *Macbeth* will focus on one or more of these aspects:

- plot and structure
- character
- theme
- setting.

In most cases, there will also be an instruction to refer to external and/or internal context in the answer.

Activity 1

It is useful to make a list of possible topics within each of these aspects so that you are confident of your knowledge and understanding. On a separate sheet of paper, copy and complete the following table. For each aspect, draw up five or six possible areas for questions. The first suggestion for each aspect is made for you.

Aspect	Possible question area
Plot and structure	Begins with witches, not nobles. Why?
Character	Macbeth: all good or all evil?
Theme	Influence of supernatural
Setting	Seven different locations: how signalled in the text?

Upgrade

An assessment question will never ask you to retell the story of *Macbeth*, nor will it require you to simply state what the characters do. Questions will always require some analysis, which you can provide by thinking about what Shakespeare's intention might have been and the effect on the audience of any particular aspect of the playwright's craft.

A very high percentage of questions on *Macbeth* will contain the words:

How does Shakespeare…

Activity 2

Explain in general terms what you need to do in your response to answer a question containing the word 'how'.

Many questions will also print an extract from the play, usually about 20 to 40 lines. Part of an answer may require you to 'begin with this extract' or 'refer closely to this extract' before going on to consider a theme, character(s) or structural aspect of the play.

Activity 3

a) Which of these qualities would you expect to see in an answer where a student had 'referred closely' to a given extract? Place a tick by all those that are relevant.

Recall of the plot from the beginning to the point where the extract comes ☐

Reference to characters not in the extract ☐   Quotation ☐

Exploration of the use and effect of a particular word or words ☐

Stating where the extract comes in the play ☐   Paraphrase ☐

Noting language effects (rhyme, rhythm, imagery) where relevant ☐

Noting how the extract fits with one or more of the play's themes ☐

Writing about what the character or characters in the extract do in the rest of the play ☐

Noting any evidence of stagecraft, or use of dramatic devices, in the extract ☐

b) The best answers will focus on language, down to the level of individual words. Add the effect of the highlighted words to these quotations below.

i.

> [I may] chastise with the valour of my tongue
> All that impedes thee from the golden round,
> Which fate and metaphysical aid doth seem
> To have thee crown'd withal.
> *(Act 1 Scene 5)*

ii.

> But now I am cabin'd, cribb'd, confin'd, bound in
> To saucy doubts and fears. But Banquo's safe?
> *(Act 3 Scene 4)*

iii.

> More needs she the divine than the physician.
> *(Act 5 Scene 1)*

Planning an answer

There are many ways to plan an assessment answer, and different methods suit different students. However, if you are writing to a time limit, make sure that you spend five minutes organizing your ideas.

Whatever type of plan you prefer (spider diagram, numbered list and so on), you need to come up with *points* and *support*. This should be a process that you practise completing rapidly.

Activity 4

Practise coming up with three points you could make in answer to these questions.

1

How does Shakespeare present the idea of the supernatural in the play?

Point 1: _____

_____

Point 2: _____

_____

Point 3: _____

_____

2

How does Shakespeare present the relationship between Macbeth and Lady Macbeth in the play?

Point 1: _____

_____

Point 2: _____

_____

Point 3: _____

_____

3

Explore Shakespeare's presentation of the ideas of greed and ambition in the play.

Point 1: _____

_____

Point 2: _____

_____

Point 3: _____

_____

In planning your answer it is useful to think of two quotations or references to events or interactions in the play that you could use to support each of your points. However, you should not waste time writing out the quotations as part of your plan. Simply make a brief note to remind yourself of the line or lines, or of the event you wish to use.

Activity 5

On a separate sheet of paper, copy and complete the table below, using your answers to the three questions in Activity 4 as starting points.

Question	Point number	Quotation/reference
1	1	1
		2
	2	1
		2

Activity 6

Now put these two planning parts (points and support) together to produce a plan for the following question. You should allow yourself a maximum of 10 minutes to complete the plan. Remember that the best answers will analyse language as well as exploring a character's function and contribution to the themes of the play.

How does Shakespeare present the character of Duncan in the play?

Extract-based questions

Referring closely to an extract is an essential skill in producing a successful assessment answer. Where there is a choice of questions, it is usual to find one that requires a focus on an extract before moving out to consider the whole play, and one that asks about the play as a whole without printing an extract.

Often, the chosen extract will highlight a particular theme or the relationship between two characters. Whatever the topic is, you will need to explore the *language* of the extract.

Activity 7

An extract from the play is printed below in two parts. This is taken from Act 1 Scene 5, where Lady Macbeth greets her husband on his return from the battle. The first part of the extract has been annotated to show how it develops the theme of appearance and reality. Continue the annotations for the second part on page 83.

Part 1

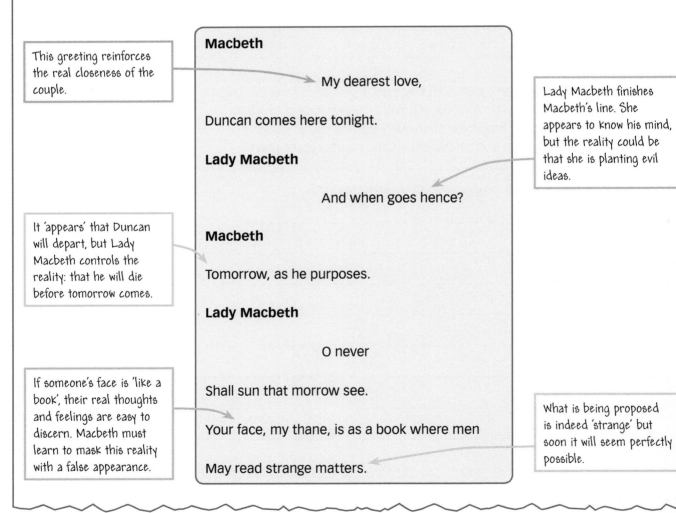

> **Macbeth**
>
> My dearest love,
>
> Duncan comes here tonight.
>
> **Lady Macbeth**
>
> And when goes hence?
>
> **Macbeth**
>
> Tomorrow, as he purposes.
>
> **Lady Macbeth**
>
> O never
>
> Shall sun that morrow see.
>
> Your face, my thane, is as a book where men
>
> May read strange matters.

This greeting reinforces the real closeness of the couple.

Lady Macbeth finishes Macbeth's line. She appears to know his mind, but the reality could be that she is planting evil ideas.

It 'appears' that Duncan will depart, but Lady Macbeth controls the reality: that he will die before tomorrow comes.

If someone's face is 'like a book', their real thoughts and feelings are easy to discern. Macbeth must learn to mask this reality with a false appearance.

What is being proposed is indeed 'strange' but soon it will seem perfectly possible.

Part 2

> To beguile the time,
>
> Look like the time, bear welcome in your eye,
>
> Your hand, your tongue; look like th'innocent flower,
>
> But be the serpent under't. He that's coming
>
> Must be provided for, and you shall put
>
> This night's great business into my dispatch,
>
> Which shall to all our nights and days to come
>
> Give solely sovereign sway and masterdom.
>
> **Macbeth**
>
> We will speak further—
>
> **Lady Macbeth**
>
>   Only look up clear;
>
> To alter favour ever is to fear.
>
> Leave all the rest to me.

Activity 8

Practise the skill of annotation on this extract. Remember to focus on the language of the extract and the effect it might have on the audience. The question is:

> In the extract below, from Act 3 Scene 1, Banquo muses over recent events. Referring closely to the extract, show how Shakespeare presents the character of Banquo here.

> **Banquo**
>
> Thou hast it now, King, Cawdor, Glamis, all,
>
> As the weird women promis'd, and I fear
>
> Thou played'st most foully for't; yet it was said
>
> It should not stand in thy posterity,
>
> But that myself should be the root and father
>
> Of many kings. If there come truth from them—
>
> As upon thee, Macbeth, their speeches shine—
>
> Why by the verities on thee made good,
>
> May they not be my oracles as well
>
> And set me up in hope? But hush, no more.

Theme-based (whole play) questions

A typical theme-based question will take the following form.

How does Shakespeare present the theme of _____ in the play as a whole?

Activity 9

a) When a question asks about the play as a whole, how many different events/ speeches do you think you should refer to?

----

b) For revision purposes, list the major themes in *Macbeth*. Look back to Chapter 5 if you need a reminder.

----

c) Take three of these themes and jot down in the table below events or speeches in different parts of the play you could use to explore the presentation of that theme in an assessment answer.

Theme	Events/speeches
1	
2	
3	

Character-based questions

It is quite usual to find assessment questions on *Macbeth* that ask about a particular character or the relationship between two characters. Almost always the question will use the phrase 'How does Shakespeare present...?' You are not being asked to say what the character does in the play; instead you should describe the ways that Shakespeare develops the character and uses him or her to further the themes or the action of the play. It is also an invitation to analyse and explore how an audience might respond to a character's words and deeds.

Activity 10

To make sure that your knowledge of the characters is secure, you should prepare brief notes on each one, together with relevant text references. Clearly some characters (for example, Macbeth) will have much fuller notes than others, but the aim is to summarize the character rather than to write exhaustively about him or her.

On a separate piece of paper, copy and complete the table below and include each of the major characters in the play.

Character name	Principal actions	Develops theme(s)	Text references

A playwright can present a character through what he or she *does*, what he or she *says* and what *others say* about him or her. Taken together, these give us a rounded character with human characteristics and failings.

Activity 11

Find three examples of things other characters say about Macbeth. Taken together, your examples should cover the full range of his character, from good to bad.

Example 1: _____

_____

_____

Example 2: _____

_____

_____

Example 3: _____

_____

_____

Activity 12

The following paragraph was produced by a student as part of an answer to the following question.

> How does Shakespeare present the character of Lady Macbeth?

This paragraph comes towards the end of the answer.

> *Although Lady Macbeth has not been seen for most of the second half of the play, in Act 5 scene 1 the Gentlewoman and the Doctor observe her sleepwalking. She seems to be going over and over the events in the past and this means that she is very troubled. It is at this point in the play that we feel some sympathy for her. This is an interesting insight into Shakespeare's skill as a playwright because he can show us how we can feel sorry for someone even if they have behaved cruelly.*

The paragraph makes several useful points and it gives the impression that the student knows the character quite well. However, there is a lack of support from the text.

Rewrite the paragraph, adding textual reference (quotation or paraphrase) to support the points made. Remember that embedding quotations is a high-level skill and should feature in your writing.

----

deduce to come to a conclusion about something that is not explicitly stated, but could reasonably be assumed

infer to work out something from evidence and reasoning

When writing about the relationship between two characters, you need of course to concentrate on scenes where they appear together, but you also need to **infer** or **deduce** points about the relationship from what the characters say about each other when they are not together.

Activity 13

a) If you were answering a question on the relationship between Banquo and Macbeth, which scenes or parts of scenes would you focus on for your answer? Make a list of the act and scene numbers (together with indicators such as 'beginning' or 'second half' if appropriate).

----

b) Annotate this extract from a student answer to identify three statements that are wrong.

> We only see Banquo and Macbeth together once but that is enough to show that they
>
> are good friends who fight together on the same side. Macbeth becomes suspicious of
>
> Banquo because he might be king one day, but Banquo never reveals any suspicions
>
> about his friend.

c) Write your opening paragraph of the answer to the Macbeth/Banquo question, improving on the paragraph above and providing an overview of your knowledge and understanding of how Shakespeare presents the relationship. Remember that you should provide a close analysis of the language used in their interactions wherever possible.

Writing successful answers: Opening paragraphs

First impressions count. The beginning of your answer should show that you are confident and knowledgeable about the topic. It may also provide an overview of what is to come in the rest of the answer.

Activity 14

Read the opening paragraph below of an answer to the following question.

> How does Shakespeare present the contrast between Duncan and Macbeth in the play?

There is a stark contrast between the 'good' King Duncan and the 'bad' King Macbeth in the play. Shakespeare emphasizes the qualities of a generous, caring king in the opening scenes (later confirmed by Duncan's son, Malcolm), but thereafter shows through actions and reports the effect that a violent and selfish king can have on his country.

This is an excellent opening. From reading it, list the points that the answer will go on to develop and explore.

Activity 15

On a separate piece of paper write the opening paragraph of your answer to the following question.

> How does Shakespeare present the character of Macbeth in the second half of the play?

Remember to provide an overview of the topic in the question and the points that will be developed in the answer.

Writing successful answers: Developing points

In thinking about how to develop paragraphs, it is useful to remember the acronym PEEL. This stands for 'Point', 'Evidence', 'Explanation', 'Link'. 'Link' is often not present, but in the best answers it looks forward either to the next paragraph or to a point that will be developed later.

Activity 16

a) Identify the PEEL structure in the following paragraph by marking the beginning of the relevant sentence with P, Ev, Ex and L.

This paragraph follows the opening to the question on Duncan and Macbeth in Activity 14.

'P' ———→ King Duncan has many good qualities. He is generous, conferring an honour – Thane of Cawdor – on Macbeth for fighting bravely, and naming his successor so that there will be smooth continuity in running the country after his death. Macbeth himself provides a testimony to Duncan's goodness when he says that Duncan "Hath borne his faculties so meek" and has been "So clear in his great office". Shakespeare makes sure that in all his appearances Duncan is seen to be acting in the best interests of others. This provides a definite contrast to Macbeth's rule.

Writing PEEL paragraphs is a skill that can and should be practised.

b) In Activity 15 you wrote the opening paragraph of an answer. On a separate piece of paper write the next paragraph, making sure that it uses the PEEL structure. Indicate the start of each element of PEEL by putting P, Ev, Ex or L at the beginning of the appropriate sentence.

Quotations

'Summing up' quotations are very useful when writing about character. These are quotations that express or sum up the most important quality displayed by any particular character.

Activity 17

a) Find one quotation that sums up each of the main characters in *Macbeth* (looking back at Chapter 3 may help). Keep the quotation short: remember that you will probably have to learn it by heart!

----

b) The same process can arm you with a set of quotations to help in writing about theme. Find one quotation that sums up the presentation of each of the main themes of the play. (Chapter 5 will help with this.)

Try to use 'embedded' quotations. This means incorporating words from the play in your own sentences. Here is an example:

> Lady Macbeth urges Macbeth to "look like th'innocent flower" in order to hide his true intentions.

Notice how the quotation fits in to the sentence without interrupting its flow. This is a high-level skill, and if done well will help to secure high marks.

Activity 18

On a separate piece of paper, take each of your character quotations from Activity 17a and write a sentence that incorporates some or all of the quotation. You should work on the basis that the sentence appears somewhere in the middle of your answer.

Now repeat the process for each of your theme quotations from Activity 17b.

Putting it all together

If you follow all the advice in this chapter, and practise frequently, you will produce highly successful assessment answers.

Below is a full answer, written under timed conditions and without access to the text. It has been annotated with some examiner's comments.

> How does Shakespeare present ideas about the supernatural in the play as a whole?

A very good opening sentence, well focused on the topic.

This statement seems to have been put in as an afterthought; it is not explained in any way.

A surprise to whom? Why should it be 'a surprise'?

Too informal for a piece of literary analysis.

This paragraph tells the story rather than providing any analysis.

It looks as though this candidate does not really understand the concept of 'equivocation' but knows it should be put in.

The supernatural runs throughout the play, casting its influence on Macbeth and to some extent controlling his actions. It is mainly seen in the characters of the witches and their prophecies but Shakespeare shows that people can be bad without the influence of the supernatural. There is also the idea of equivocation in the play.

The play opens with the witches. This sets up the idea that the supernatural is in control of everything. The witches know that they are going to 'meet with Macbeth', which is a surprise. Shakespeare is showing us that there are forces outside of nature that know the future. Their first set of prophecies get the ball rolling, but mostly because Macbeth tells his wife about them and she decides to make sure that they come true.

The second entrance of the witches shows them as much more nasty. The spell they make up is full of disgusting ingredients and they use this as a spell to make Macbeth see 'apparitions' that tell him another set of prophecies and set up what he does in the last part of the play.

Of course, the witches only tell the truth at the beginning so that Macbeth believes them. But their later prophecies have double meanings, which brings in the theme of equivocation. It turns out, for example, that Macduff was born through caesarian section so he wasn't strictly 'born of woman' and can therefore kill Macbeth. Finally Macbeth realizes that he has been tricked:

> *That keep the word of promise to our ear*
>
> *And break it to our hope.*

The play was performed for King James, who was interested in witchcraft and the supernatural. To please the king, Shakespeare goes along with the idea that witchcraft is real, but he shows how it doesn't win in the end.

A useful idea, but it is not developed later in the answer.

It is a rather big assumption to state that a short opening scene ('This') shows the supernatural in control of everything. It would be clearer to say that 'This' emphasizes the importance of the supernatural in the play.

The point that human actions are sometimes as instrumental as the supernatural could be developed here.

The quotation is not properly introduced and makes little sense as it stands.

Bringing in the historical context, which is useful, but the end of the answer is not strong.

Activity 19

a) Looking at the full answer on page 91, what further points would you make in your own answer to the sample exam question, bearing in mind what you have learned about the play and how to write about it? Write your answer on separate paper.

b) Overall, the answer has several good ideas in it, but these are not always well-explained or supported. Redraft the answer on separate paper so that it displays the skills covered in this chapter and is clear, well argued and well supported. Incorporate the points that you have noted in Activity 19a.

Activity 20

Below are three questions on the play that might appear in an assessment. For each question, plan and write a full answer. If your course requires writing under timed conditions, aim to complete each question in no more than 45 minutes (up to 10 minutes planning and 35 minutes writing).

1 How does Shakespeare present and use the witches in *Macbeth*?

2

Lady Macbeth

What beast was't then

That made you break this enterprise to me?

When you durst do it, then you were a man.

And to be more than what you were, you would

Be so much more the man. Nor time, nor place

Did then adhere, and yet you would make both.

They have made themselves and that their fitness now

Does unmake you. I have given suck and know

How tender 'tis to love the babe that milks me:

I would, while it was smiling in my face,

Have pluck'd my nipple from his boneless gums

And dash'd the brains out, had I so sworn

As you have done to this.

(Act 1 Scene 7)

Starting with this speech, show how Shakespeare presents the character of Lady Macbeth in the play.

3 How important is the theme of appearance and reality in the play?

Progress check

Use the chart below to review the skills you have developed in this chapter. For each column, start at the bottom box and work your way up towards the highest level in the top box. Tick the box to show you have achieved that level.

I can sustain a critical response to *Macbeth* and interpret the themes convincingly ☐	I can use well-integrated textual references from *Macbeth* to support my interpretation ☐	I can analyse the effects of Shakespeare's use of language, structure and form in *Macbeth*, using subject terms judiciously ☐	I use a wide range of vocabulary and can spell and punctuate consistently accurately ☐
I can develop a coherent response to *Macbeth* and explain the themes clearly ☐	I can use quotations and other textual references from *Macbeth* to support my explanation ☐	I can explain how Shakespeare uses language, structure and form to create effects in *Macbeth*, using relevant subject terms ☐	I use a range of vocabulary and can spell and punctuate, mostly accurately ☐
I can make some comments on the themes in *Macbeth* ☐	I can make references to some details from *Macbeth* ☐	I can identify some of Shakespeare's methods in *Macbeth* and use some subject terms ☐	I use a simple range of vocabulary and spell and punctuate with some accuracy ☐
Personal response	**Textual references**	**Language, structure, form**	**Technical accuracy**

Glossary

ambiguity   using words or phrases where the meaning is not clear, and where something can be interpreted in different ways

blank verse   poetry that has iambic pentameter but does not rhyme

catalyst   a person or a thing which starts or speeds up a series of events

climax   the highest or most intense part of the play or a turning point in the action

declaim   to pronounce words loudly and clearly in a precisely articulated manner

deduce   to come to a conclusion about something that is not explicitly stated, but could reasonably be assumed

equivocator   someone who uses words or phrases with more than one possible meaning in order to be evasive or misleading

exposition   key information to help the audience make sense of the action and characters in the play

falling action   the parts of a story after the climax and before the ending

figurative language   language that uses figures of speech, is metaphorical and not literal

flaw   a fault or weakness that makes an object or person imperfect

function (of character)   the part a character plays in moving along the plot or highlighting a particular theme or themes

iambic pentameter   a line of verse with ten syllables, where the stress falls on the second syllable (and then every other syllable) in the line

imagery   visually descriptive or figurative language

inciting incident   an action, event or conversation that sets the plot going

infer   to work out something from evidence and reasoning

irony   a literary technique where the intended meaning differs from what is said or presented directly

metaphor   the use of a word or phrase in a way that is not literal, for example, Duncan's planting and nurturing metaphor in Act 1 Scene 4

motif   a word, phrase or image in literature that is repeated to create specific effects. Note that this is slightly different from a recurring *image*, where different words may be used to evoke the same word picture.

nihilism   believing that life is meaningless; refusing to believe in any moral principles

offstage   taking place in the area of a stage that is invisible to the audience or in a location not seen that the audience must imagine

ominous   a warning sign that something bad might happen

prose   any writing in continuous form without rhythm or rhyme

protagonist   the leading character in a play, novel or film

pun   using the different meanings of words, or their similar sounds, to create an effect, often humorous but sometimes startling

resolution   the ending of a narrative where problems are solved and matters are concluded

rising action   a sequence of events that builds towards the climax

simile   a comparison of one thing with another, using 'as' or 'like', for example, "signs of nobleness like stars shall shine" *(Act 1 Scene 4)*

soliloquy   where a character voices aloud their innermost thoughts for the audience to hear

symbolic purpose   the use of a character or object to represent a quality or theme (for example, goodness or truth)

theme   a significant idea that recurs in a poem, play or novel

trait   a person's distinguishing quality or characteristic

upstage   the area towards the back of the stage

usurper   someone who seizes the crown without the right to do so

verse   a group or series of groups of written lines, containing a rhythm or rhyme

OXFORD
UNIVERSITY PRESS

Great Clarendon Street, Oxford, OX2 6DP, United Kingdom

Oxford University Press is a department of the University of Oxford.
It furthers the University's objective of excellence in research, scholarship,
and education by publishing worldwide. Oxford is a registered trade mark
of Oxford University Press in the UK and in certain other countries

British Library Cataloguing in Publication Data

Data available

ISBN 978-019-839884-4

10 9 8

Printed in Great Britain by CPI Group (UK) Ltd., Croydon CR0 4YY

Acknowledgements

The publisher and authors would like to thank the following for
permission to use photographs and other copyright material:

Cover: © Maggie Brodie/Trevillion Images

Extracts are from William Shakespeare: *Macbeth*, Oxford School
Shakespeare edited by Roma Gill (Oxford University Press, 2004)